THE MAKING

Trust God to be the Chairman of Your Boardroom

Dionne L. Grayson

The Making: Trust God to be the Chairman of Your Boardroom

Copyright © 2020 Dionne Grayson
All rights reserved. No part of this book may be reproduced or transmitted in any form or by any means without written permission from the author.

Scriptures marked NIV are taken from the NEW INTERNATIONAL VERSION Copyright© 1973, 1978, 1984, 2011 by Biblica, Inc.™. Used by permission of Zondervan.

Scriptures marked NKJV are taken from the NEW KING JAMES VERSION (NKJV): Scripture taken from the NEW KING JAMES VERSION®. Copyright© 1982 by Thomas Nelson, Inc. Used by permission.

Scriptures marked TM are taken from the THE MESSAGE: THE BIBLE IN CONTEMPORARY ENGLISH (TM): Scripture taken from THE MESSAGE: THE BIBLE IN CONTEMPORARY ENGLISH, copyright©1993, 1994, 1995, 1996, 2000, 2001, 2002. Used by permission of NavPress Publishing Group.

Scriptures marked ESV are taken from the THE HOLY BIBLE, ENGLISH STANDARD VERSION (ESV): Scriptures taken from THE HOLY BIBLE, ENGLISH STANDARD VERSION ® Copyright© 2001 by Crossway, a publishing ministry of Good News Publishers. Used by permission.

ISBN: 978-1-952327-00-1
Library of Congress Control Number: 2020903592
Printed in the United States of America

T.A.L.K. Publishing, LLC
talkconsulting.net

Table of Contents

FOREWORD i
PREFACE vii
THE MAKING EXPLAINED 11
KNOWING YOUR WHY 23
SWEET SPOTS, DEVELOPMENTAL SKILLS, AND BURN OUT SKILLS 27
WHERE IT ALL BEGAN 31
GOD'S FIRST CHOICE 35
CAPACITY BUILDER AND NEXT LEVELER 39
YOU'RE ON TO SOMETHING 45
GOOD IDEA 51
GOD IDEA 55
NO LONGER MOVED 59
AFRAID? DO IT ANYWAY 65
YOU BETTER LISTEN 75
TRUST THAT HE GAVE IT TO YOU 79
KNOW THEM THAT LABOR AMONG YOU 87
THE NEED TO KNOW 91
CONCLUSION 95

DEDICATION

It is with great pleasure that I dedicate this book to the loving memory of my mother. Cassandra Shaw was the best gift God could have shared with me. Thank you, mom, for being such a beautiful example of integrity, virtue, and strength.

FOREWORD

THE MAKING: TRUST GOD TO BE THE CHAIRMAN OF YOUR BOARDROOM

If you were to ask the average person, "What is the greatest nation on earth," you would likely receive a wide array of answers. Many would likely engage in the mental exercise of trying to match outward accomplishments of contemporary times, such as technological advancement(s), as well as the marvels of antiquity, like the great pyramids of Egypt and the like, in search of valid proof of said national greatness. However, no matter what geographic area, territory, or time mentioned, it would be incorrect – for, the greatest nation on earth, is **'IMAGINATION,'** and it serves as a function of the spirit inside every person. Its greatness lies in its transcendent, boundlessness of vision, space, and time. What one can conceive – in his or her imagination – one can achieve. The unfortunate reality is that most people do not look inwardly often or long enough to extract precise answers and remedies to challenges they face in life, personally or professionally.

In her masterpiece, *The Making: Trust God to Be the Chairman of Your Boardroom,* author Dionne Grayson takes the reader by the hand on a journey of inward exploration to extract the best answers – those given by God – for every challenge one may face at any given moment in time. Through an examination of the trials and triumphs of King

David from the Bible, coupled with a peek into her journey through life's defeats and victories, Dionne weaves a compelling tapestry of the benefits of following God's lead to the winner's circle time and again. And the beautiful part about it is that God will use your makeup, disposition, and sometimes, even scope of previous experience to orchestrate more significant outcomes on your behalf.

In an age where educational attainment can tout as the pinnacle of knowledge acquisition, the notion of inward or spiritual guidance often is despised – if considered at all – as the best source for solutions to problems at the most critical times of decision-making. Nevertheless, given the 'inner-man' houses our thoughts, feelings, and emotions, it stands to reason that it's from that inward place that our most accurate answers to life's questions and challenges should emanate. Moreover, Proverbs 20:27 informs us that,

> "The spirit of man is the candle of the Lord, searching all the inward parts of the belly."

What this means is that God himself speaks to us, impresses upon us and leads and guides us through our spirit or, said another way, through our inner man. As such, it behooves us to consult our inward 'self' for insights and the best answers from God for any given circumstance or situation in our personal or professional life – or in this case – boardroom.

I've personally experienced the benefits of following God's lead inwardly on many occasions. On one such time, I was serving as Public Affairs Liaison for my church, and we were in search of a building in which to conduct weekly worship service(s). Having served as chief of staff to a City Council President, as well as a lobbyist representing varying interests locally, statewide, and on Capitol Hill, I was familiar with the governmental apparatus. However, in this particular instance, the Pastors of the church were led to one specific community wherein services would be conducted and had retained legal counsel to interface with the government officials regarding our property search. The officials of this community were not welcoming. When my Pastors applied for an occupancy permit for the building they identified as 'the one' and reached an agreement with the property owner to lease the building, the government officials denied the occupancy permit application returning the application fee. How's that for a welcome mat? We eventually were granted a hearing before the Mayor, City Administrator, and the Common Council of this community to state our case for why we wanted to be in the community and why we should receive an occupancy permit. Although not designated as the lead spokesperson, in the days leading up to the hearing, the voice of God spoke to my inner man and told me to prepare a presentation to appeal to the government officials of the resistant community. My initial thought was, "our legal counsel is charged with this task," but I obeyed the voice of God and prepared a presentation of appeal, making a case for our approval.

When we got to the hearing, the physical set-up of the committee room was designed to be intimidating. The officials were perched up about four or five feet above the gallery and podium from where the applicant would make their case. Up until that point, the officials had refused even to accept our occupancy permit for review. When it came time for our legal counsel to present our case before the officials, the attorney became flustered by the atmosphere, room set-up, and precise feedback received from the officials. As I witnessed what appeared to be our opportunity to present a compelling case for approval slipping away, I got up from my seat and asked the presiding chairman of the hearing if I could speak on behalf of my Pastors. I nodded to our legal counsel in a way to indicate that I'd take over from here, was granted permission to speak, and then proceeded to lay out our case in a 10-15 minute presentation – just as God had instructed me to draft days before. After the hearing, the City Attorney came out into the hallway to greet us, complimented me on the presentation, and informed us he would set up a meeting. The meeting with the City Attorney would consist of our team, himself, and a separate property owner. Its purpose was to secure an occupancy permit to conduct weekly worship services in that community, which we did for several years.

The above account of victory resulting from following God's lead is what Dionne lays out in this book. I have known Dionne for over a decade, and she has been exemplary in walking out the premise she lays out in *The Making*. In a world increasingly inundated with more and more information, receiving a download of 'winning' information from God is even more critical. I invite you to absorb the tenets of this book and allow God to be the chairman of your personal and professional boardroom. Your decision-making and quality of life will be better for it.

Tim McMurtry II
President, Tim McMurtry International, LLC
Associate Pastor, World Outreach Center (W.O.C.)

PREFACE

As we journey through this book, know that your gifts are for the world, and you are more than qualified to give birth to them. God planted a seed in you, and he expects that you will give birth to that seed. Having a seed does not mean "challenge free living" or "entirely as planned." There is work required. The seed will manifest if you move forward. Imagine for a moment a woman who is pregnant, but when it comes time for her to give birth, she cries out, "I cannot do this; I am not qualified to give birth to this baby!" As onlookers, we'd view her oddly because we would see the physical manifestation of a carried seed, knowing she is capable of giving birth. We would also see all she needs to do is push. With giving birth, pain is inevitable, and there may even be fear or complications along the way. However, for the baby to enter the world, the fact remains the one carrying the baby will have to bear down and push.

For any vision, dream, or desire to manifest, pushing is a requirement. To push means to exert force on something or someone to get it away from where you are. As it relates to what God has placed within you, He expects that you will recognize what is there and do the necessary work to pull it from within. He desires to see what's in you impacting the world around you. The question becomes, what is stopping you from pushing? Why is it that some people walk in their gifts and talents, and others do not? Is it fear? Do they not know how? Is it feelings of inadequacy? If you are struggling with any of the previously mentioned, particularly feelings of inadequacy, whether you realize it or not, God has equipped you with everything you need.

> *I can do all this through him who gives me strength.*
> (Philippians 4:13 NIV)

You will benefit from walking in your area of gifting. However, the one who stands to gain the most is the benefactor of the gift—those waiting on what you will offer. Once you begin to move forward pushing, fanning the inward flame, and placing a demand on the gift inside of you, watch what happens! The process is all part of *The Making*. Your making, my making, our making, as we are growing to walk boldly in what God has called us to do in business.

This book will share stories of my personal experiences encountered while navigating business decisions. I will candidly share outcomes favorable and not so favorable, times when I listened to the voice of God and those times when I did not. As you read through these stories, I'll refer to David, a shepherd boy who became the King of Israel. As an emerging leader, his life was an excellent example of triumphs and challenges often encountered in business. In *The Making*, I share what I learned as a businesswoman revealing strategies used with the principles discussed. Lastly, the boardroom discussions at the end of each story are there to challenge you to make changes necessary to help you navigate everyday business decisions.

The boardroom is where you have candid discussions with God and He directs you in everyday situations. It is where growth occurs. As you read this book, be brave, be honest, and write out what you need to perfect. Your participation is an example of the push required to walk confidently in what you will do to have success in business.

THE MAKING EXPLAINED

As I share my journey in becoming an entrepreneur, I want to give you a glimpse into my position during those experiences. I hope you will gain an understanding of how you can navigate challenges and decisions while at the same time, successfully navigate your business. Using our example of David, who the bible calls a man after God's own heart, we see that David loved God; he spent time with God and had unwavering confidence in His presence being with him. As we encounter triumphs and challenges with business decisions, interactions with clients, and engagement with our staff, there is a posture we can take that will aid us in being most effective. I call it *The Making*.

If you ever wondered how having a relationship with God correlates with faith and business, you are holding the right book. In *The Making*, I will share simple stories with corresponding actions I am confident will resonate with you. *The Making* is where your most significant success lies. It is where you decide to push through challenges because you know there is purpose. Where after each push, you find yourself getting more strength. It's where battles, great and small, are won. *The Making* is what we do when no one is looking, the behaviors that produce personal thriving and professional success. It's not a mere visitation with God during a Sunday service, but it's taking Him home with you, allowing Him to be the Lord of your life and business daily.

In David's tenure as a shepherd, he stood up, taking full advantage of challenges and opportunities. With his encounter with the giant Goliath, David allowed what was inside of him to navigate the situation before him.

What David possessed was so real that it caused a stirring whenever a challenge or opportunity presented itself. David's confidence in confrontation didn't develop overnight. Over time, he adapted consistent behaviors that eventually led to him becoming a great warrior and leader.
Let's look back for a moment and see what caused a young shepherd boy to be bold enough to stand up and take advantage of an opportunity to move swiftly through military ranks working with Saul, the King of Israel.

SHEEP TENDING

> [32] *David said to Saul, "Let no one lose heart on account of this Philistine; your servant will go and fight him."* [33] *Saul replied, "You are not able to go out against this Philistine and fight him; you are only a young man, and he has been a warrior from his youth."* [34] *But David said to Saul, "Your servant has been keeping his father's sheep. When a lion or a bear came and carried off a sheep from the flock,* [35] *I went after it, struck it and rescued the sheep from its mouth. When it turned on me, I seized it by its hair, struck it and killed it.* [36] *Your servant has killed both the lion and the bear; this uncircumcised Philistine will be like one of them because*

> he has defied the armies of the living God.
> ^{37} The Lord who rescued me from the teeth of the lion and the paw of the bear will rescue me from the hand of this Philistine."
>
> 1 SAMUEL 17: 32 – 37 (NIV)

David had an overwhelming confidence in God's ability to prepare the way for him. His firm trust in God developed out of spending daily, quality time with God. While tending sheep, David talked to God and sang Him love songs in worship. Every day he wrote psalms and played music worshipping God. Can you imagine how full of God's presence David became? No internet, no television, no social media, just he and God. I can imagine God conversing with David and David experiencing God's loving presence, as he was lying beneath the clouds by day and the glistening stars by night. I envision the hot, yet calming wind blowing and David experiencing the Lord's sovereign love in the dry Middle Eastern breezes.

Your perception of challenges and opportunities change when you experience God, as David did. You see yourself from God's perspective recognizing that each worship encounter infuses your life with God's character. It stirs something inside that's usually unable to be contained. It manifests itself in your daily navigation. From his writings in the Psalms, we see that David was dependent on God and relied on Him in his decision making. This young shepherd boy relentlessly pursued excellence when no one was watching by the simple act of tending to his father's sheep.

This truth brings me to the first tenant of *The Making*, *Sheep Tending*.

Sheep Tending is the preparation time that occurs while no one is watching. Seclusion is the place where our relationship with God, ethics, and integrity begins to develop. Integrity creates habits for our daily engagement with large and small decision making. When David was alone with the sheep, and a bear or lion tried to attack the flock, his instinct was to kill them. When David heard of Goliath threatening the army of Israel, the same instinct that led him to kill the lion and bear, caused him to volunteer to kill the Philistine. There is a practical and spiritual side here. David spent time in worship and talking to God, and in the natural, when conflict arose, he was ready for it. He tapped into what was inside of him. David fought lions and bears when they tried to infiltrate the flock, and in doing so, was preparing to be one of the greatest warriors of all time. David did not become a warrior when he became officially part of Saul's army. He became a warrior in a field tending sheep when he chose to fight off what tried to kill the flock entrusted to his care. Imagine for a moment, David submitting to fear and climbing in a tree for safety, instead of saving the sheep. What if he completely ignored the potential that lay in his relentless pursuit of excellence while tending sheep?

David did not have to contend with the enemy of the sheep, nor the threat to the nation of Israel, he could have run away in fear, giving the lion and bear access to ravage the sheep and Goliath access to destroy Israel. Like David, you don't have to contend with the Philistine giants of life—those circumstances that seem greater than your desire or ability to handle. But what processes or systems become compromised? What's lost because of your decision, or who becomes prey if you don't? What can be ravaged by a refusal to contend with giants perceived or real in your life or your business?

Imagine what would happen if you faced the enemy and fear head-on, and the growth it would present to you personally and professionally. What is waiting for you on the other side of fear? Is it a promotion? Is it growth in your business? Is it increased morale for your employees, or clarity of direction and vision for the corporation? The demolition of fear causes a chain reaction that will affect the entire trajectory of your business goals. Do not be afraid of the perceived Philistine giants in your life. They are all part of *The Making*.

GOD CONFIDENCE

> [4] *A champion named Goliath, who was from Gath, came out of the Philistine camp. His height was six cubits and a span.* [5] *He had a bronze helmet on his head and wore a coat of scale armor of bronze weighing five thousand shekels;* [6] *on his legs he wore bronze greaves, and a bronze javelin was slung on his back.* [7] *His spear shaft was like a weaver's rod, and its iron point weighed*

> six hundred shekels. His shield-bearer went
> ahead of him.
> 1 SAMUEL 17:4 –7 (NIV)

Looking at Goliath's stature, his armor, and battle experience, David had every right to be fearful, but he refused to be. David walked in the second tenet of *The Making*, *God Confidence*. *God Confidence* is a disposition that comes after a decision to trust in God confidently.

With *God Confidence*, you do not allow your insecurities or fears to make decisions for you. Instead, you mentally transition to the truth that God is with you and will always go before you, and you act and maneuver as though He has. *God Confidence* empowers you to look past what you see around you, trusting what God has on the other side– Success. David looked past Goliath's height, his full armor, and even the fact that his armor-bearer was carrying his shield before him. What Philistine giant do you need to look past in business? What person, decision, or emotion is keeping you from becoming who you have the potential to be?

USE YOUR OWN TOOLS

> Then Saul outfitted David as a soldier in armor. He put his bronze helmet on his head and belted his sword on him over the armor. David tried to walk, but he could hardly budge. David told Saul, "I can't even move with all this stuff on me. I'm not used to this." And he took it all off. Then David

> *took his shepherd's staff, selected five smooth stones from the brook, and put them in the pocket of his shepherd's pack, and with his sling in his hand approached Goliath.*
> 1 SAMUEL 17: 38 – 40 (Message)

When we are in *The Making*, we carry tools, gifting, etc. to navigate life and business. God will use what he has invested in us at specific times. When he speaks to us, His instruction may seem strange to others, but he knows what's in our arsenal; he knows our armor. Although it may be impractical, theoretically, or politically incorrect, we will succeed if we listen. I am confident that many of us have success stories of instances where we made a decision that went against the grain. Those times we used what we knew best to receive the desired outcome.

The third tenet in *The Making* is *Use Your Own Tools*. One of the greatest demises of any leader is trying to walk in someone else's shoes. David cultivated his strength in battle using the wisdom of God and his bare hands. Saul wanted David to fight his way, with traditional weapons of war. What would have happened if David had stepped before Goliath wearing Saul's Armor? Imagine not only the ridicule to the nation of Israel of David's defeat because he chose armor unsuited for him, but also consider the amount of strength David would have exerted wearing Saul's heavy armor. By the time David would have reached the Valley of Elah, Goliath would have killed him because David would have been too exhausted to fight the battle.

What tools has God given you? What has he told you to do that you may be using someone else's ways to do it?

Do not try to look like, talk like, or be like anyone else. Doing things as God designed you to do it is all that's required. Remember, the world is waiting for you to do things exactly the way God told YOU to do them. Doing things God's way is what the world wants and what the world needs to see and experience from you. If you copy or mimic another person, the authentic benefit will not be afforded to others because you have chosen to be a counterfeit. David's tools were his hands, a sling and five smooth stones, what's in your toolbox God can use to help others?

BELIEVE, SAY, THEN DO

"Come on," said the Philistine. "I'll make roadkill of you for the buzzards. I'll turn you into a tasty morsel for the field mice." David answered, "You come at me with sword and spear and battle-ax. I come at you in the name of God-of-the-Angel-Armies, the God of Israel's troops, whom you curse and mock. This very day God is handing you over to me. I'm about to kill you, cut off your head, and serve up your body and the bodies of your Philistine buddies to the crows and coyotes. The whole earth will know that there's an extraordinary God in Israel. And everyone gathered here will learn that God doesn't save utilizing a

> *sword or spear. The battle belongs to God—he's handing you to us on a platter!"*
> 1 SAMUEL 17: 44 – 47 (Message)

Your adrenalin should be in full swing right now. This scripture is incredible and brings me to the 4th tenant of *The Making, Believe, Say, Then Do*. David believed God was with him, and God would deliver Goliath into his hands. David said, speaking directly to King Saul, Israel, and Goliath exactly how things would turn out. He believed it, he said it, then David took action by killing Goliath. Not once when David fought Goliath, do we hear where he referenced himself with deficiencies. David was young, a shepherd boy, history tells us that David was much shorter than Goliath. He didn't have traditional armor, nor was he professionally trained at war, David wasn't even part of the army of Israel. But David heard from God. He knew God would grant him victory. He believed it, declared how things would turn out, and we know what happened next.

David's victory over Goliath brought him great fame and notoriety. Unfortunately, it also brought intense jealousy from King Saul. The people of Israel loved David. After the battle with Goliath, they began publicly showing love and appreciation for David, and they even compared his feats with that of the King's. The people's praise of David made King Saul very angry so much so that Saul sought ways to assassinate him. David had to run for his life.

CAVE EXPERIENCE

> ¹ *So David left Gath and escaped to the cave of Adullam. Soon his brothers and all his other relatives joined him there.* ² *Then others began coming—men who were in trouble or in debt or who were just discontented—until David was captain of about 400 men.*
> *I Samuel 22: 1 – 2 (NLT)*

The fifth and final tenet of *The Making* is *Cave Experience*. Every leader will find themselves in a cave –a place of shelter for seclusion or security. David didn't go into the cave willingly. He was trying to preserve his life. What David did not know, however, is the *Cave Experience* was the next level of preparation needed to rise as King. God blessed David with his presence, and he carried it wherever he went. Even while David was running for his life, hiding in caves, that blessing rested upon him, and his favor with God and men grew. People followed David even when he was a fugitive. The numbers following David grew so large they formed an army of nearly 400 men who became known as David's Mighty Warriors.

While in the cave, David knew fear gripped his men, but instead of hosting a pity party with them, David resorted to doing what he always did, worshipping the Lord. David and the men sang songs taking their eyes away from their circumstances, placing them where they needed to be, on the Lord. The entire 34th chapter of Psalms is said to be the songs David and the men sang in the cave at Adullam.

I will bless the Lord at all times: his praise shall continually be in my mouth. My soul shall make her boast in the Lord: the humble shall hear thereof, and be glad. O magnify the Lord with me, and let us exalt his name together. I sought the Lord, and he heard me, and delivered me from all my fears. They looked unto him, and were lightened: and their faces were not ashamed. This poor man cried, and the Lord heard him, and saved him out of all his troubles. The angel of the Lord encampeth round about them that fear him, and delivereth them.
Psalm 34:1-7 (KJV)

David was very intentional about leading his troops to a place of strength, and he did it through worship. David's strength came from the Lord and kept him moving forward, empowering his army to become the best. *Cave Experiences* are like diamonds formed under intense heat and pressure. It's what makes us who we are. *Cave Experiences* take the pressures and stresses of leadership and transform us into who we ultimately will be as developing leaders.

KNOWING YOUR WHY

Your why is that thing which causes you to act. Your end goal, the big picture. Sometimes called your North Star, your purpose— the reason you do what you do. It causes you to rise when others are sleeping; it's the consistent practice of a skill you work on perfecting, it's the thing that causes you to stay awake at night as you think of strategies to get tasks accomplished. Your why produces impetus reaching an end goal—knowing your why also serves as an inner gyroscope, which is a device used to measure or maintain your relative position. Your why will keep you abreast of where you are relative to your dreams and visions. It is what determines the activities you engage in, the decisions you make, and how you live your life.

> *Each of us has a why, something that motivates us. My "why" is helping people walk in their gifting and purpose.*

When I see individuals, especially the young operating in their area of gifting, it elicits excitement. My heart palpitates, I become moved with emotion, and there is a literal stirring that occurs in my inner being. It's essential to pay attention to what elicits passion or excitement in you. It's not always the smiles and positive feeling that move us to bring about our why sometimes it's things that anger us, or the need for change. That is our why.

For me, the frustration of what I did not receive as a teenager preparing for life after high school fueled my life's work. I wasn't an A student, nor did I get in trouble, so I went under the radar. I was of the group never given opportunities traditionally provided by the guidance counselor and some teachers. I remember transitioning to college and asking God what it is that He wanted me to do. I asked with all sincerity. I wanted to be sure my college experience was meaningful. This answer did not come overnight. I switched majors three times, attempting to find my passion and my why. After discussing my situation with my aunt, I'll never forget her simple prayer. She said something like this. "Lord, we ask that you open the doors so wide that Dionne has no choice but to walk through them. Those things that are not you, please close those doors to her. " In my sincerity and pursuit, God began to open wide doors of opportunities for me to start working with young people. I also received an award as someone with the POTENTIAL to impact Milwaukee's youth. Someone saw my potential to work with young people before I began or could even see it in myself.

Some of you have skills and talents no one knows about, things housed in a protected, secret place. Most do. Pay attention to your secret place, the things you do in private. What happens in those times when what's in you is consciously or unconsciously revealed? You may sing your heart out while at home in the company of family or alone. You may serve as an excellent chef, preparing meals and delicacies for loved ones. Or perhaps you sew for your children and people rant and rave at how the clothes are comparable to a renowned fashion designer. Even yet, you give the most compelling speeches in front of a crowd of one and rock the house. Please consider that you are working on something. From your protected place, in your quiet, relentless pursuit of excellence, you are perfecting your gift.

Maybe you never viewed those things you do well as a business, a source of revenue, or even a gift to others, but I assure you it is if you allow it to be. Be brave enough to show the world what that is. Believe it or not, there is a designated group waiting to experience what you are privately perfecting.

Boardroom DISCUSSIONS

What is your secret gift? What is that thing you do in private not many know about, or maybe no one knows?

Share that gift with someone this week and talk to someone you trust about it and see what happens.

SWEET SPOTS, DEVELOPMENTAL SKILLS, AND BURN OUT SKILLS

I want to encourage you to do some self-examination. Take time to evaluate your participation and engagement with work, service, as well as your extra-curricular activities. As you are preparing to walk boldly in what God called you to do, let's make sure you are operating in the right space. Do a simple exercise looking at sweet spots, developmental skills, and burn out skills.

Wiktionary defines a sweet spot as *any place that is optimal for obtaining a certain desirable effect or result*. These are skills you love to engage with, those you excel in effortlessly. Your sweet spot is where you should spend your time. It can be in a traditional full-time position or a venture you have yet to begin. For me, my sweet spots are program development, strategic planning, capacity building, and coaching.

Developmental Skills are those skills you enjoy using but haven't fully developed. This skill is where you should be spending most of your time. If you want to be a public speaker, take advantage of every opportunity to speak. In your relentless pursuit of excellence, create an outline, research your topic, practice speaking, and then talk. Enroll in a class, seek a mentor or coach. Do what is required to develop in those areas. You will only get better when you practice and say yes to opportunities to do so. Volunteering is an excellent and safe way to put to use those skills you need to build. When offered opportunities to hone your development skills, be brave, stand up, and take advantage of the opportunity. Some of you may have to go back to opportunities that you said no to and say yes. For me, my developmental skill is public speaking.

Burn out skills are the skills you are excellent at, and people ask you to do them frequently, but you no longer enjoy doing them. These skills need to be delegated or eventually removed from your life because they exhaust you. They require a great deal of mental preparation. They are easy to pinpoint because they are often those skills you find yourself complaining about and anxiously anticipating the work to be over. Continual engagement will not only ruin your physical health but affect your emotional health and wellbeing.

My burnout skills are administrative, scheduling, creating resumes, etc. I did it professionally and proficiently for years. But to operate in these areas today would be excruciating and exhausting. Start saying no and bow out gracefully. You are now occupying another individual's seat. Focus on your sweet spot, spend time honing your developmental skills, and move to your next phase of growth.

David, a shepherd boy who became King of Israel, stood before his brothers and King Saul, to fight the giant Goliath. At the time, no one knew privately he was a protector and warrior, no one but David. When David mentioned fighting Goliath to his brothers and the King, neither thought he was capable, nor was he considered to take on the challenge. Eliab, David's older brother, felt his presence was ill-intended and told him to go back to tending sheep.

When you know you are excellent at something, show up, don't ask to be there, confidently walk in what you are to do.

David knew his *why*. He excelled at taking care of sheep and was a great warrior. David did not equate his responsibilities as a shepherd to ruling a kingdom or becoming the leader of a nation. He just knew his sweet spot, relentlessly pursued it with excellence, and eventually became one of the greatest kings of Israel.

Boardroom
DISCUSSIONS

In the space provided below, list your sweet spots, developmental skills, and burn out skills.

While making a list, be honest, and write out the appropriate skill in the respective section. Do not allow fear to dictate what you write on the line. It does not necessarily reflect what others think of you or how they see you but how you see yourself. After you make a list within your sweet spots, circle a skill you can commit to work towards. Next, circle a developmental skill you will commit to working towards enhancing. Finally, remove yourself from all activities that involve your burn out skills. Once you begin to make these changes, you will be on a path of intentionally pursuing your why.

Sweet Spots:

Developmental Skills:

Burn Out Skills:

WHERE IT ALL BEGAN

After graduating from Alverno College and participating in an internship, the Volunteer Center of Greater Milwaukee hired me as their Youth Program Director. I was excited. Here I am on the path of exploring the fascinating combination of serving as an administrator and partnering with young people. My responsibility involved developing a youth program that creatively engaged young people in volunteerism. A year into my post, I had a minimal budget to hire a small team. Because I did not have enough dollars to hire a full-time person, I used those dollars to provide part-time jobs for two teenagers, Annie and Montique, who would help me manage the program.

I recall an instance where I had to travel for a week-long conference with the Corporation for National Service. This mandatory conference occurred at the worst possible time for our program, and I had no choice but to leave two 10th graders in charge of managing my affairs while traveling. We met several times before I went and discussed all that needed to be taken care of while I was away. Now, mind you, the assignments I shared with them were real tasks that were part of my full-time responsibility. When we met, they both assured me everything would be okay. While I was away, I did not receive any phone calls from the young ladies, and as you can imagine, not knowing was challenging. When the trip was over, and I came into the office on the following Monday, I braced myself for what I was about to learn and set aside time to fill in unmet gaps. However, in the meeting, I discovered that these young ladies handled the day to day operations of managing the department, and they also accomplished some very productive additional tasks. At that moment I didn't know how to feel. Should I be intimidated by these two, or could I take a step back and realize that this was a good thing?

I envisioned the worst and prepared myself to work extra hours. Annie and Montique helped shape how I engage with young people. I'm so proud to say that our program, with the assistance of two 10th graders, gained national recognition on three occasions to include coordinating the nation's largest National Youth Service Day. It would not have occurred had I not been open to the power of allowing these young ladies to flourish. It was an early lesson learned while developing as a leader.

THE MAKING

I could have looked at this situation in two ways. I could have fed the moment of insecurity, and it could have turned into a very unhealthy *Cave Experience*. Imagine if I had chosen to posture myself the way King Saul did when David was rising in popularity for his victories throughout Israel. Instead of continuing to develop David as a leader, Saul was in great turmoil resulting in him consistently trying to kill David. Please know this, you will struggle to grant opportunities for development to someone you feel is a threat to you. The girls were excellent, and I prepared the space for them to cultivate their gifts. Instead of submitting to a quick insecure emotion, I chose to tap into and train young people by constructively engaging them in real-life work experiences. This principle is what led to my youth development philosophy and how I co-founded a successful non-profit organization with 22 young trailblazers nearly fifteen years later.

Boardroom Discussions

Is there a situation that you need to look at differently? What is in the way of a different perspective for you?

Identify it and do the work to change your perspective.

GOD'S FIRST CHOICE

You learned a bit about my tenure at the Volunteer Center. That job was a foundational experience. I am grateful for the responsibility and flexibility entrusted to me to develop the department and its people. It is where I learned to apply my love for administration and to work with young people. As a young adult, I was not aware of how there could be such an intertwining of the two.

> *I was beginning to experience the practical side of walking in purpose.*

I loved my job; it provided many opportunities for me to get to know non-profit work, and much of what I did was a first for me. It was my first job out of college, and I learned how to write grants, raise funds, facilitate meetings, engage with the business community, and plan large-scale events. After three years of serving, I came across an opportunity that spoke very loud to me. Now, I wasn't looking for a change, change found, and spoke very clearly to me. When I saw it, I knew in my heart; this is for me, designed with me in mind. I believed it, and I said it out loud because I knew it was my next step.

I interviewed for the position, was hired, and developed programming that gained city-wide recognition. The program became a model and training site for new employees in respective locations across the city. I truly thrived in the position. Attendance was high, community members were engaged, and I continued to see growth in the young people we served. I share this because, later into the position, I learned that in the eyes of the interviewers, I received the job by default. Let me explain. One gentleman was offered the job but later declined. After he turned it down, a second gentleman accepted the position but, a few days later, also changed his mind. Of course, it was very disheartening to the interview team. They settled with me because I was the only option left, and they could either start the interviewing process over again or offer the position to me. They chose me. Reluctantly, but they decided on me because of time, so they thought.

I had a choice at that moment when I learned this information. I could either take offense feeling insecure about the fact that the interviewers didn't want me in the position, or be excited that although I wasn't their first choice, I was God's. And because I was God's first choice, I was selected, and I thrived.

THE MAKING

Do you see a pattern here? *The Making* is full of practical choices. It shapes how you position yourself when you engage with others and receive information. I refused to be upset when I learned the additional hiring facts. It honestly brought great comfort and excitement, knowing how God navigated a situation because I was His choice. I believed the position was for me, perfected my resume, and applied for the job. God went before me, but I had to do my part (*Believe, Say, Then Do*) to walk through the door.

Boardroom DISCUSSIONS

If you are anything like me, which I believe you are, you feel something stirring inside you that you need to move on. If this is the case, I want to serve you notice that your time has officially expired to continue to sit with it.

Write it out below. Believe, Say, Then Do.

CAPACITY BUILDER AND NEXT LEVELER

The company I manage today, Building Your Dreams, was born in 2003 as an LLC. It was not intentional on my end; I didn't set out to be an entrepreneur, nor did I have a desire to be self-employed. I honestly didn't know that entrepreneurship was a thing. It was something that evolved over time. I recall being terminated, one job after another. Each termination was due to no fault of my own. Looking back, I now know my time had expired with traditional full-time employment opportunities.

> *I had to do something different, and God had to position me in such a way that I could see it.*

I can personally share that being terminated is an awful feeling, especially when you know decisions were a result of unfair treatment. I hit a rough patch, unemployment, and feelings of insecurity. I cried a bit. But I could not stay there long because I knew there was a next. These incidents drew me closer to God. It was a low place; a place of financial struggle, insecurity, and feelings of unworthiness mainly because I didn't understand why or what was next. I entered an unfamiliar place. People showed up at my house with groceries. I'd receive phone calls from people asking me to meet them at the gas station so they could fill my gas tank. This season turned out to be a tremendously humbling experience. But I had to learn to be okay with receiving. You see, I am a giver, accustomed to being on the giving end, this was all new for me.

During *Cave Experiences*, you want to be sure to protect yourself by staying in God's word and keeping individuals around you who are only speaking positivity to your situation. If you are not careful, this season can be where you make devastating mistakes, so keeping things in perspective is critical. I don't recommend big moves during these times.

To gain clarity, I went on a 30-day fast and began to ask God pressing questions. I reviewed my resume and my experiences. In the process, I noticed I only stayed on any particular job 3 – 4 years and then moved on to the next. This revelation made me wonder why I didn't have staying power. However, God showed me my involvement in the job entailed creating, building capacity, and taking the position to the next level. Once accomplished, I moved to the next project.

I did not realize that I was a capacity builder and a next leveler. While on the job, I'd build infrastructure and level up programming. After this realization, I thought about how I could make this work to my advantage. As I was coming off of my fast, I had this new sense of direction. I knew I wanted opportunities to help individuals, small businesses, and nonprofits build. I now had a focus. I knew what to look for, what questions to ask, and how to present myself when among individuals. It wasn't long before I obtained my first, second, and third contracts. When I received my first contract, I spent a week getting myself ready, forming my official business. I registered for an EIN, purchased a domain, got my marketing materials together, and anything else necessary to legitimize my business. When someone googled, I wanted people to find me and work with me. When God made this clear, I made a very conscious decision to move forward excellently. Whatever God has impressed upon your heart, just start, do something. Educate yourself and seek advice. As you move forward, people, opportunities, and experiences will present themselves. Trust and walk in the leading of God, and he will guide you in all things.

THE MAKING

Realize that where you are today is nothing more than a stepping stone to where God will take you tomorrow. If you could see your life down the road five, ten, or even twenty years from now, you would be surprised to find how God, down through the years, has strategically moved you from one place to another. Even in those times when you may have moved around unwillingly. You didn't realize that in some instances, the agony of a termination gave birth to building your God-given dream. But it did, and in the process, God has given you the tools necessary for his ultimate plan for your life. David had no idea that while he was taking care of his father, Jethro's flock, killing a lion and a bear that one day he would be taking care of God's people protecting the entire nation of Israel. Every situation David found himself in before assuming his role as King would add more tools to his leadership toolbox. It's why we can never despise the days of small beginnings or the places we may find ourselves. God may be using that temporary place to build a permanent skillset in your life as a businessman or businesswoman.

Boardroom DISCUSSIONS

Do you feel like you are at a critical juncture in your career? What is truly in your heart to do?

Spend some time reflecting, fast if you need to and allow God to show you what your next step is. Don't get stuck, the answer is usually in front of you.

YOU'RE ON TO SOMETHING

Once I learned I was a capacity builder and "next-leveler," I solidified contracts I enjoyed, and they served as the epitome of me walking in my gifts. I recall one summer in my early twenties when a gentleman came to my office while at the Volunteer Center, and he asked me to help him find volunteer placements for his students. I, of course, assisted and offered to find service opportunities that interested students career-wise. This thought came from my experience with Annie and Montique (the 10th-grade students from the Volunteer Center), coupled with the idea of a curriculum I designed and taught while in graduate school. A few months later, the gentleman called back and asked if I'd be interested in talking to his supervisor about teaching a service-learning class and finding volunteer placements for their students. I, of course, agreed.

When I spoke with his supervisor, something happened during our conversation. He did a traditional interview to get to know me and afterward asked, "Would you be willing to teach the class?" It was a pivotal moment. I had another idea in my heart I wanted to present. It was something I loved doing, and I knew it would better align with their program goals. I could either agree to teach what he proposed or share the idea I had for students to explore careers. I pitched it, he accepted, and I began teaching the class at a major university.

Now, this assignment was a "making experience." While teaching, I was *Sheep Tending*. I developed great passion and conviction around what I was teaching. I took it seriously, and it was by far my absolute favorite thing to do. In nine years of teaching three sessions each week, I was never late to class, nor did I ever cancel. I showed up an hour early for each session because I wanted to be there for my students when they arrived. I wore my best attire on class days, spent time preparing for each class, and I kept my word with my students. This contractual assignment honed a work ethic, discipline, and love for teaching in me that is still alive and evident today.

I can recall a summer where I found internship placements for all of our students, except for 11 who were interested in exploring careers in the health field. After hours of searching, I received an opportunity to meet with the Chief Medical Officer at a Health Center, Dr. James. Although they would only host 2 - 3 students, I was determined in my heart and knew if she met the students and had the opportunity to talk to them, she'd host them all. I confidently spoke to what appeared to be a Philistine giant of a situation, and I told that giant what it was going to do.

The day arrived when I finally met Dr. James. You can imagine at such a young age, I was initially very intimidated to talk to a woman of her stature. What could I possibly say to her that would convince her that she should host students? What could I propose that would help her feel compelled to provide an opportunity for those interested in health careers?

> *I got rid of the negative feelings, and it gave way to my God Confidence.*

I knew what was in these young people, and I knew she would not regret providing an opportunity for them to serve. When we met, I don't recall her ever looking at me while talking, and she acted as though my very presence was an irritant to her. She busied herself working on something else and appeared to be half-listening to my conversation. Even in her seeming disregard, deterring me was not an option. I knew this might have been my only shot at getting placements for my teenagers, and I was confident she would concede. Summer vacation for the students was about to begin, and I did not have another option. Although her demeanor said otherwise, she agreed to meet with the students and said she wouldn't make any promises. That was enough for me. I saw an open door!

When the day for interviews came, Dr. James was more than 2 hours late because of complications with a patient. But the students and I waited. While waiting, I called her assistant, who assured me she was still coming. When she finally arrived and interviewed all the students, she came to me asking who prepared the students. My students stood out. I trained them to be confident young people, well equipped to meet any interviewer. For some reason, when she asked, I deflected the compliment and shared that the students were part of a pre-college program and went on to share about the program. She politely interrupted me and said, "No, my dear, who prepared them for this experience with me today? The things they said in their interviews, who taught them that?" Eyes wide opened and a bit stunned, I politely said, "I did ma'am." She leaned over and looked in my eyes, pointed at my face and said, "Stay right there; you are on to something; I'll take all 11 students."

Dr. James proceeded, "I never encounter such preparedness with young people." She started working on moving another group that she committed to and inserted our students instead. That was over 15 years ago, and her words of affirmation stuck with me and are the reason I created and scaled the *Dream.Explore.Build.,* experience. I was operating out of pure passion and a love for sharing vital information that our young people were hungry to have, critical developmental skills I didn't receive as a teen. I loved what I was doing, but the thought had never occurred to me to take it beyond where it was. Dr. James planted a seed that put me on a path of empowering more than 1,000 high school graduates, and the best is yet to come.

THE MAKING

There are a few examples here of *The Making*. What I want to focus on is my mindset while teaching the class. There was no way for me to know that I'd be working on a curriculum that would develop into a monetized program offered throughout our city's high school educational institutions. My attitude and actions stand out as an example of the pursuit of excellence. It started with a graduate school assignment I completed with excellence, which led to my mindset while teaching (being on time and wearing my best attire, etc.), and eventually led to a city-wide signature program. This process began in 1998 as an internship exercise. It did not evolve overnight. When you are in *The Making*, you cannot sprint through the process. It is difficult and impossible to run at a fast pace throughout a marathon. When you rush, there are many things you will not be able to experience. While in a marathon, you allow for ethics and good character to form in you that only come with time.

Boldness, faith, and tenacity in my heart, mind, and spirit could only happen over time with more than one opportunity to develop.

Be honest with yourself. What can you say you haven't done excellently?

What can you commit to doing that will shift your mediocre outcomes to the excellence you are destined to operate in?

GOOD IDEA

As I reflect on my career, I absolutely love how things have pieced together. The challenges and triumphs were all prepared for the very next step of my why. I appreciate the beautiful building blocks God has built to aid me to develop into a tenacious, confident professional, and the opportunity to grow in some areas I needed as a person first, then as a professional.

I recall taking on a three-year contract. My responsibilities included developing and training frontline staff and their managers. As you can imagine, this was my sweet spot. It was the intersection of so many things I love to do. I also discovered some new skills and became passionate about them, as well. I took up the charge to provide quarterly training for managers and their support team members. I also coached individuals within their roles. My office was a safe place to learn, share, and receive the support needed to be effective in one's respective position. I quickly learned that if you take an interest in an individual's big picture and connect it to their role, they'd be most effective and have a vested interest in the company. I wanted to be effective in my position, which ignited a desire to get a coaching certification. This certification was not part of my contract, so I had to fund it myself.

It did not take long for the recognition of my work by the president of the organization. One day, his secretary reached out to me and requested a meeting on behalf of the president. We had a lunch meeting at a country club, and during that time, he attempted to get to know me better and find out my overall strategy and goals around my role. The meeting ended with an offer of a vice president position. No interview, no defined job description, he just knew he wanted me in that role. I thanked him for the offer and told him I would think about it and give him an answer when I returned from the certification training. The program training was in Florida. After arriving, I unpacked, changed clothes, and went directly to the pool area. I had to have a conversation with God. I chose the pool because being near water is where I have my best conversations with God. I was looking for answers, and I needed them before I left that weekend.

My training experience was outstanding! As I was learning coaching practices, I was excited and couldn't wait to get back to begin working one-on-one with individuals so I could help them build capacity in their respective roles. Day 1 of the training passed, and I hadn't received an answer from God about the vp position. Day 2, still no response, Day 3, nothing. Day 4 arrives. This day, the master trainer, the one who created the certification, was teaching the class. While training, he deviated just a bit and began talking about monetizing your coaching experience. He shared the benefits of being self-employed and how you can be productive in your delivery because you don't have the distractions that often come with having a full-time job.

Everything he said resonated with me. I hung on every word. While talking, he was walking around the room. He stopped in front of me continued to teach and after a moment, he said, "The challenge with being a contractor is everyone wants to hire you because of how effective you are." If you can imagine, he piqued my interest. While standing in front of me, he pointed right at me and said, "When offered those positions, your answer is no!" Imagine my excitement! I might have had a second thought if he was standing across the room. But he stood right in front of my table and pointed directly at me. God had answered me. I knew God was speaking through my instructor. My answer was crystal clear, and I handled the situation accordingly when I returned home. I did not accept the role of vice president.

THE MAKING

There is such a thing known as a good idea and a God idea. With one the rewards come at the top, out the gate, you see the benefits, but with the other, it requires a walk of faith. A good idea is an opportunity that makes sense and aligns with you. A good idea can often provide a space to use your gifts and talents. A God idea, on the other hand, can appear to be the opposite. Initially, it can be confusing appearing to be "off purpose," but if you follow God's direction, it will yield more favorable outcomes than a good idea. The president of the company offered me a good idea; I was qualified and am confident I would have thrived, but I would have been off purpose. God called me to be an entrepreneur.

Boardroom DISCUSSIONS

Do you have an opportunity tempting you that appears to be a good idea and not a God idea?

What is the opportunity? I want to encourage you, only to take what positions you to advance in your God-given mission in life.

GOD IDEA

Contracting and being an entrepreneur was something I truly enjoyed and was very much in alignment with the lifestyle I desired. I chose the individuals I wanted to work alongside. I partnered with several organizations for mutually beneficial experiences. Vacation and sick days were a thing of the past. I was able to craft my life in a way that allowed for meaningful work and many vacations. During this time of contracting bliss, a mentor unexpectedly asked me to apply for a position he concluded was a good fit for me. In the spirit of keeping my interview skills sharp and out of respect for the person who recommended me, I interviewed for the position with absolutely no intention of accepting if offered. After the interview, something unexpected occurred.

I received a phone call offering me the position. I was honestly disappointed about this offer because I had no intention of taking on a full-time job. While on the phone, I was speechless and told the individual offering the position that I needed a few days to think about their offer. I had become accustomed to multiple streams of income, and this position would force me to push my mission aside, not only ending major contracts but also engage with moving the vision of another organization forward.

They offered four weeks of vacation and a designated number of personal days. Additionally, the pay was significantly lower than I was making self-employed. That in itself was reason enough not to take the position. Before declining, I prayed and made sure my decision was a God one. For some odd reason, although not what I wanted, I felt a sense of peace at the idea of taking the job, but I wanted to be sure, so I called my dear friend in Las Vegas and asked her to pray with me. After prayer, my friend confirmed, the job was indeed for me, and went on to say, Dionne, the position isn't about you; it's bigger than you." She confirmed what was already in my heart. What a complete and total curveball. I have to say I was very disappointed and I attempted to negotiate the offer made to me. How do you make the transition from the freedom of being an entrepreneur to punching a clock and income caps? My negotiation was without success, but I knew I had to take the job because God was leading me to do so.

He is the manufacturer of my life; he knows what he is doing, even when I don't.

So out of obedience to the Lord, I took the position, and I was allowed to open doors for many people and create opportunities that would not have been had I not been in that place. When my time was up, I transitioned, and words I spoke just a few years prior were beginning to manifest. The same place I didn't want to work, hired me to start a non-profit organization with 22 young trailblazers that would later be the site for the program I desired to scale citywide— the same one presented to Dr. James many years prior. Had I not taken the position, organizations, groups, and individuals would have missed opportunities. Because I said yes, I was able to experience the manifestation of words I spoke just seven years prior.

THE MAKING

Are you praying about your decisions? Are you allowing God to order your steps even when it looks unfavorable or favorable? Do the moves you make align with what God has already shown you and what you prayed about? When you evaluate opportunities, be sure that you are selecting God's ideas and not merely good ideas.

Boardroom DISCUSSIONS

What decision do you need to make that requires you to pause and ask God for direction?

I want to challenge you to consult God and be sure that your decision is in alignment with what He shared with you.

NO LONGER MOVED

When I walked into the room, there were dignitaries, flags from other nations, beautiful ethnic garments, and people who appeared to be significant. Backs upright and dignitaries, greeting one another with very pristine bows. I was escorted around the room and introduced to lovely women from other nations who served as ambassadors.

When asked what country I was from, the person who invited me said, "This is Dionne Shaw, and she is from the United States."

Although I felt somewhat intimidated by the experience, this day would, however, turn out to be very pivotal. It was the last day of a 30 day fast, and I needed some clarity. I was serving in a very coveted full-time position and had no desire to continue in that role. I loved how God placed me in a spot where I could open doors, provide opportunities, and have a voice at important tables. But I wasn't happy. I would sit in the parking lot, sometimes in tears, because I did not want to go into the building. Power, privilege, and racism were at the forefront of my experience, and I was exhausted with those interactions.

I recall a meeting with a client very vividly, and one of the women I met with was very visibly disgusted with the fact that she and her supervisor, who were both Caucasians, were coming to me for assistance. She resented me and the authority I represented. She was rude, condescending, and her face was in complete alignment with how she felt. The conversation was intense. Her supervisor had to interject on a few occasions so we could get through the meeting. It was horrible, and nothing got accomplished because she could not get over the fact that it was a young black woman who was in a position to assist her. This negative encounter was just one of many battles experienced with no support from my employer.

One day I questioned God and asked why. "Why can't I just quit this job and move on to whatever was next?" I was very emotional about it. I had to work hard not to allow how I felt to translate into the work I was doing each day.

Usually, when I prepare for a significant career shift, opportunities would be a literal phone call away. I was accustomed to having available opportunities as well as those designed with me in mind. Not this time, after many requests, no one had a position or a contract to offer me. So again, I asked God why? "Why can't I just transition right now?" No answer.

I continued to ask the Lord why, in my unhappy state. Each day I walked into the office, I repeated the question. During my questioning, situations continued to become more complicated. Once I was reprimanded for doing something authorized by my supervisor. His authorization led to he and I both being openly criticized before the company president and others. The level of disrespect and dishonor displayed to us both bothered me, and I honestly struggled. When God finally answered my question, he said to me in an oh so sweet language, one He knew I'd understand.

> *"You'll be moved when you are no longer moved."*

That is not what I wanted to hear. However, I knew then I needed to get my emotions intact and effectively maneuver this transition and not be emotional about it. I knew my days were numbered. I also knew I had to be fully present to receive what God had for me during my final days. I certainly didn't want to miss it and did not want to revisit situations like the one I had encountered. I had to learn how to deal with challenges and not be overtaken by emotion.

Now, in this room full of dignitaries, I eventually gained confidence and began to engage and realized that these were people just like me, those God positioned to be in authority. I had another engagement, so I had to leave early. The person who invited me said to me on my way out, "Do not get stuck. Your position is coveted and not the end; I want you to see bigger." In tears, I said, "You have no idea the magnitude of what you just stated to me." That conversation was the other piece of my release. I submitted my resignation, was confident, no longer moved in my emotions, and several doors opened to include my employer hiring me for a significant project as a contractor. The challenges I faced while employed by this company afforded me a chance to grow in areas that were not possible while working as an independent contractor.

THE MAKING

Do not allow your emotions to be the decision-maker for you. Trust the process and let what needs to be groomed in you to develop. While at this temporary place of employment, I had the means to leave my post, and I also had the desire to leave the position abruptly. I also had an overwhelming proven confidence in God that would not allow me to make a move without His guidance. When you find yourself in these types of positions, take a step back, get your emotions intact so that you can maneuver with a clear perspective. This type of maneuver requires you to be completely honest with yourself and not make decisions when your emotions are dominating.

Boardroom
DISCUSSIONS

What elicits emotion in you in business? It could be anger, hurt feelings, jealousy, or even fear. Whatever it is, learn not to take things personally and navigate through them.

Once you identify it, pay close attention and manage your emotions and how you handle situations with the Word of God.

AFRAID? DO IT ANYWAY

Years ago, I received a congratulatory email that stated I received an award for outstanding contributions to the community. This recognition was undoubtedly a pleasant surprise. It was an honor to be selected with other exceptional women for this award by a group I admired.

When the day arrived for the ceremony, I got dressed and was very excited to attend and be in the presence of so many inspiring women. Upon arrival, I was ushered into a reception room and given a quick orientation. During the orientation, they congratulated the women and shared the ceremony agenda. They ended by stating that after receiving the award, we would have 1 minute to speak. Hearing that statement made my face go stone cold. Speaking was not part of the plan, and I certainly was not informed of this before the ceremony. My heart dropped, I felt a massive ball of dry cotton in my throat, and everything around me went numb.

After the orientation, I could not hear anything said, nor did I focus on understanding the remainder of the necessary instructions because I was so afraid. I was now required to make an acceptance speech.

This emotion had me so tied up in a knot that I couldn't enjoy the food, didn't talk to the other guests, and I walked around the space rehearsing in my head what I would say. I honestly thought of ways to escape that situation altogether. I even remember going into the restroom stall, taking deep breaths to calm myself down because I was terrified of speaking in front of this massive group of people.

Fear is crippling; fear is a dream killer; it will cause you to miss out on opportunities making things appear real that are not. A good portion of my life, I've battled fear. It became a mode of operation. It determined how I engaged with people and became part of my personality. I've missed opportunities, been at tables where I had a voice that I didn't use. In relationships, I wasn't honest because I had information that would help resolve or clarify, and I didn't share because of fear. I finally got to a place where I became sick of myself, and this thing called fear had to go. Fear would no longer be a significant part of my life.

I knew I needed to do something about fear because I didn't want to continue missing out on business opportunities, relationships, or life itself. I began a journey to learn about fear. What is this thing I allowed to torment me in my sleep, accompany me at work, and rule in my everyday actions?

1 John 4:18 (NIV) reads,

> "There is no fear in love. But perfect love drives out fear because fear has to do with punishment. The one who fears is not made perfect in love."

I heard the story of a man talking to his neighbor, and his young daughter came outside and stood next to him. While standing there, the neighbor's dog came out because he wanted to be near his owner. When the little girl saw the dog, she immediately tugged at her father, motioning for him to pick her up. Now I imagine the little girl was shaking just a bit and her heart was racing because she was afraid of the dog. I can even believe she hugged him tight once he picked her up because she knew she'd find comfort with her father. After a few minutes in her dad's arms, something interesting began to happen. First, the daughter started staring at the dog, then she began to reach down to touch the dog, and eventually, she was able to stand on the sidewalk playing with the dog. What happened? From the moment the man picked up his daughter, she became confident and was comforted by the love of her father. Her confidence in his love dissipated the fear, which enabled his daughter to do what she couldn't do before.

The story had a significant impact on me and broke something within me that changed my life to this very day. I realized I needed to get closer to my heavenly Father and spend less time rehearsing and giving place to fear. In the Message Bible, 1 John 4:18 begins with God is Love. When we take up permanent residence in a life of love, we live in God, and God lives in us. I needed to work on developing a closer relationship with God, our Father, so that I could have the confidence of the little girl.

God is love, and when we allow him to be who he is within us, fear dissipates. How can we be fearful when love is in us? At that moment, I reconnected with God as my loving Father because I realized how much time I was spending on my deficiencies and not His love. I had to learn to make God so big in my life that I was no longer concentrating on fear. I learned that the gifts God gave me are to be used for the betterment of humanity. How can I help others if I am afraid to release what I have openly? It's a part of my calling. I am gifted with abilities, talents to encourage, build, and uplift. How dare I question my manufacturer? That is what I was doing. From that moment forward, I began to study who God was rather than spending so much time focusing on fear.

So back to this event. As you can imagine, I wasted a great deal of time worrying instead of enjoying myself because I was battling with a crippling feeling. When it came time to line up award recipients, I prayed something like this. "Father, I cast my care on you because I know you care for me. You brought me here for a reason, and I pray that you give me the words to say so that the people here are blessed." In that moment of sincerity, when I made God more prominent than the fear, those feelings dissipated, and I was very confident in who I was in Him.

Sitting on that stage, *God Confidence* kicked in. I stopped preparing in my head, enjoyed the ceremony, and entirely relied on the Lord to give me what to say. When they said my name, I walked up to the microphone very confidently. I had no clue as to what I was going to say. To this very day, I do not remember what I said, but a little over a year later, I ran into a woman I didn't know who thanked me for the words of encouragement. She stated that she needed to hear what I said that day.

THE MAKING

When a situation arises, and you have a chance to back out because you are afraid. Don't back out, do it anyway, allow *God Confidence* to kick in. Make up your mind that you will not miss out on any opportunity because of fear. You have to practice combating fear, or you will become accustomed to submitting to it, creating sabotaging habits. Remember, each time you submit to fear, you are allowing it to become more prominent in you. When you confront it, you see it for what it is. Every encounter with fear builds more strength to combat it, and before long, it has no choice except to dissipate.

Have God's Word in your arsenal to use when the feeling of fear arises. Those like:

> *"There is no fear in love, but perfect love casts out fear. For fear has to do with punishment. The one who fears has not been perfected in love."*
> 1 John 4:18 (ESV)

This verse reminds us to lean into God's love, that he's bigger than fear, that he has enabled us with every tool necessary to be a success in life. There are no inadequacies in the love of God because He is with us.

> *"I know what I am doing, I have it all planned out – plans to take care of you, not abandon you, plans to give you the future you hope for."*
> Jeremiah 29:11 (Message)

That scripture reminds us that in business situations, God brought you and me there, and He knew what He was doing when He opened the door, presented the opportunity, or provided the introduction. We no longer question it; we walk in it.

> *"I can do all things through Christ, which strengthens me."*
> Philippians 4:13 (KJV)

This scripture clearly shows that we have the ability and the power to accomplish every feat set before us.

As you see, eliminating fear requires a real-life relationship with the word of God.

Here's a confession to make when you feel afraid:

God created me for this,
He has equipped me for this opportunity
God knew I would be here at this moment;
he had it all planned out.

*I am fearfully and wonderfully made in His image
no one can do this as I can.
I will go and do what God has called me to do,
and I will do it with excellence.*

> This kind of attitude and actions only happens when we look fear in the face and continuously do what fear says we cannot.

When you oppose fear it:
- solidifies your humanness and magnifies your need for God
- raises the conqueror in you
- propels you to move past what is in front of you
- creates tenacity and drive in you

Fear is one of the top reasons people don't follow through on the call God placed upon their life. Grow past fear, so it is no longer a deterrent in walking out what you know you a designed to do; what others are waiting on you to do.

To experience victory at the ceremony, I had to look fear in the face and confidently do what it was telling me I could not do. Not preparing a speech was an action that said God I rely on you. In that place, God meets us, and He's always faithful. The danger is when you do the opposite; YOU provide an open invitation for fear to not only live on the inside of you but to fester, create anxiety, and a host of other emotions and become more significant in your life as much as you allow. Never pass on any opportunity tremendous or small because of fear.

Boardroom DISCUSSIONS

Pick one thing that you are afraid to do, confront, or change.

Once you identify it, make up your mind that you are going to confront and change it. Write what you perceive to be the Philistine giant in your life and what you need to do to stare it in the face so that you can begin the process of dissipating it. Find a scripture that speaks to it and meditate on it until you see change.

YOU BETTER LISTEN

As you learned earlier, Dr. James planted a seed that affirmed and ignited the journey to train young people to be very passionate and intentional leaders in an ever-evolving global workforce. The process continued with me teaching for nine years, updating, testing, and improving a curriculum. I also had a desire to offer the experience citywide. Yet, I did not know how to go about making this happen. When my term ended at the university, I was saddened by the thought that the program would no longer be available. As mentioned previously, this was my absolute favorite thing to do, and it met a great need with the young people I felt called to serve.

Nearly six years later, I was home about to walk up the stairs in my condo, and I felt an overwhelming, compelling feeling to call a particular city official and meet with him to share a proposal I was submitting to a foundation. To my surprise, before calling him, I received a phone call from his office requesting that I be part of a task force he was forming. It was a God moment. After he initiated his invite, I asked to meet with him to discuss my proposal. He mentioned that he was going to be on vacation for a month and would meet with me once he returned. In my heart, I knew it had to occur sooner. Although apprehensive, I got a bit more assertive and stated I wanted to share something with him that I am confident would change the face of workforce development for young people in the city of Milwaukee. He paused, and there was a moment of silence, then he told me to come into his office that week. I prepared for the meeting and presented the idea to him. What I appreciated most is he listened intently and asked very thoughtful questions. The meeting ended abruptly due to an emergency. Two days later, he called, stating that he loved the idea and had spoken with the Mayor. I received seed money to launch the program citywide. This new venture was unexpected. I was merely obeying what I believed to be the voice of God and a firm direction within me. I had no clue how it was going to unfold; I simply obeyed.

THE MAKING

What is the lesson? Follow your instinct and never allow fear to stop you. As previously stated, when an opportunity comes, do it even if afraid, do it afraid. It takes courage, and if you move forward, you will continue to develop in that area. Had I not had the courage to seize the opportunity as David did with Goliath, I would not have launched the program, nor would I have impacted the lives of hundreds of young people in the city.

Boardroom DISCUSSIONS

What is something that your instinct is telling you to do? It could be a phone call, a meeting, or a connection.

Whatever it is, write it out here and work towards it.

TRUST THAT HE GAVE IT TO YOU

As previously stated, there were times the Lord told me to do something in business that did not make sense theoretically or practically. I would, at times, share with my team the direction I received, only to have people later request private meetings to share their concerns. They would inform me that my plan wasn't the norm and it did not make sense. I received statistics, case studies, and local stories of others who tried. They attempted to prove my idea was not the best way.

> *Although I knew what God shared with me, I decided to empower my team and follow their lead.*

After all, they would be the ones executing what I was sharing. I can honestly say that the few occasions I listened to the team when I had that leading from God, resulted in some form of loss. A loss in funding, program quality plummeting, a compromised peace of mind, and even partnerships aborted. I did the opposite of what I instinctively knew to do. It was a great lesson learned.

THE MAKING

Please remember, God gave what you possess to you. He shared the vision, idea, concept, and big picture with you! It won't make sense to others, and they cannot see it because He did not give it to them. It should not frustrate or intimidate you when they don't understand. Trust God's leading and remember He knows best. He designed you to do what you do the way He gave it to you. Do your research, and do not make frivolous decisions. When you decide, be informed, know that you know.

Boardroom DISCUSSIONS

Have you ever known in your heart that you were supposed to do something a particular way, but did it another?

What problems did that cause for you? How did you fix it? What are some steps you can take to be sure you use your tools and not someone else's?

TRUST THAT HE GAVE IT TO YOU – HERE WE GROW AGAIN!

No, this is not a mistake; the title is repeating itself because this is an area that needs perfecting for many. Here we grow again!

When you start a new business, non-profit or for-profit, the first few years are always tough, especially when you are forced to expand and hire staff to help with the vision. I experienced this a few times, and it was exciting and extremely challenging at the same time. Growth is inevitable, and when you expand past your startup team, the rules are different. We had an opening for a critical position and interviewed several qualified candidates. I selected the individual most skilled at what I needed. There was no comparison between their skill set and the others interviewed.

I also interviewed another candidate who happened to be a college intern currently working at the organization. They had great potential, operated in integrity, and we worked together beautifully. The college intern didn't have the skill set of the other individual but certainly had the potential to grow into it. When presenting the candidates to the board, I leaned more toward the individual I worked well with, the one who demonstrated the potential to be successful in the position. There was an inner peace when I considered them. My board of directors strongly cautioned me against hiring my choice. Although in my gut, I knew this wasn't what I knew to do.

I did not have peace, but I went with the board's decision and, unfortunately, paid handsomely for it. Yes, the individual was highly skilled, but they were also tough to work with and caused discord amongst the team. It was so complicated that we never had the chance to cultivate our working relationship. This individual was not a fit, and I knew it before they arrived. Their time of employment was very short-lived, and after the termination, I couldn't go back and make an offer to the college intern because they moved out of town. That was a painful learning experience that kept me in God's face. Although I didn't listen that day, I knew better moving forward.

THE MAKING

Sometimes we make the same mistakes and expect different results. We all know if you want change, you have to do something different. We can't run away from what needs developing. Be brave, trust the growing process.

Hiring practices are an area that in time I developed, painfully, but I did. Trust your instinct. Once you hire people, spend time helping them evolve in their roles. Find out what they want to do and align their work, respectively. Joel Manby has a book entitled *Love Works*. It is an excellent resource for managing individuals and helped me walk in love with challenging employees and contractors.

Boardroom DISCUSSIONS

What area of business do you keep making the same mistakes?

Write it out here; discuss what you have to do to make changes. Now that you have it written out, read bible scriptures that will help you and ask God to show you how to navigate.

KNOW THEM THAT LABOR AMONG YOU

The Bible says to know those who labor among you (I Thessalonians 5:12). In business, this means to not only know their skill set, aptitude, and weaknesses; it means to know their character, tendencies, and, most importantly, their heart. I can recall having an employee in a leadership position who knew I was one who leads by listening to the Lord, even though I did not verbally articulate it to them. When God tells you something, there is a confidence, a swag if you will, that no one can take away from you. You know whatever He shows you is going to work because He gave it to you. That is confirmation of success. You are just required to take action and move towards it. The manufacturer who is God gave it to you. That means you will have guaranteed success. Why? Because you have the equipment. The previously mentioned employee always knew when God told me something. Her demeanor when I spoke was in tune, and there was a different level of response in her actions. She respected me, and she never questioned what was requested. She jumped right in and flowed because, in her heart, she knew God was at work. When you have this kind of synergy with your employees, it creates a fantastic team experience, environment, and a desire for people to want to get to know God. Because I saw how she followed God's leading, I began to engage her in what God was showing me, and as a result, we experienced tremendous growth in the organization.

THE MAKING

I want to encourage you to get to know your employees, vendors, and superiors. God will guide you and give you wisdom with those relationships. It's one of the keys to removing toil from your business. It does not have to be turmoil and struggle. We can have healthy working relationships in our offices if we take the time to get to know people and cultivate the best experience for them while accomplishing company goals.

Boardroom DISCUSSIONS

What can you do to make your workplace better for others? For your subordinates? How can you be a better employee?

Take actions towards making it better. Write out what you can do here.

THE NEED TO KNOW

I cannot tell you how many times I've heard people say, "I wish God would show me how this is going to turn out. I need to see the big picture." or "Why won't He tell me more?" I want to put you at ease with wanting to know EVERYTHING all at once.

I am a planner, one who is very analytical, so not knowing things ahead of time was challenging for me. I'll share an occurrence that made me so appreciative of how God loves me and already has plans for me.

I signed up to participate in what's known as an Author Lab hosted by T.A.L.K. Publishing. The Author Lab helped me to write this very book. Leading up to the lab, I had nothing to write. Nothing was flowing, and I felt as though this process wasn't for me. Information was fluid for the other authors, but it wasn't for me. These thoughts left me feeling unexcited to participate, and I honestly had to push myself on the idea of even being there. Had I gone off of how I felt, I would not have participated in the experience. Something beautifully unexpected occurred when I walked into the first lab. I sat down, fully embraced the worship music that was playing, and I began to write. God walked with me through the entire experience and gave me what I needed when I needed it, no toil.

THE MAKING

The weeks leading up to the first day of class were hectic for me, and I honestly could not handle any new information that wasn't connecting to what was I was currently engaged with. But God not only gave me what to write when I needed it, He also presented it at a time I could handle it. The truth is, I wasn't mentally prepared for the information before the day I received it. I did not have the bandwidth to take on another task. That simple act of receiving the information at the Author Lab created a greater confidence in me knowing that God will give me the next step when it is time, I am ready, and it is appropriate.

Boardroom
DISCUSSIONS

Are you anxious? If so, about what? Take a deep breath and do what you know to do. It can be as simple as getting an EIN and making a vision board. Take the first step, and as you take it, the next step will be clear. There is a music video by the late Michael Jackson called Billie Jean. In the video, Michael is walking and dancing down the street, and as he takes steps, squares light up to show him the way. As he moves forward, the next step lights up. Nothing happens until he moves. Rest securely, take a step, and the next will illuminate.

Write down what you are anxious about or an area you lack patience. Find a scripture that will help you through the situation.

CONCLUSION

Critical and strategic conversations with God are what helps to move your business or non-profit forward. I trust my stories serve as examples of how you can receive the best counsel around your everyday actions in business. I hope something resonated with you, that you pay attention to your heart and mind as you make day-to-day decisions and respond to challenges. Take full advantage of *The Making*. Know that *Sheep Tending* is a central place; it is where you acquire the basics of your business acumen. Once you allow yourself to grow while *Sheep Tending*, you have no choice but to *Believe, Say, Then Do*, and *God Confidence* will automatically emerge. Allow God's Spirit to speak to you, and when you receive the best outside counsel, be sure it is in total alignment with what God is saying to you. Be confident in that knowing. If you are going through a *Cave Experience*, pray, go to the Word of God, pick up this book, and remind yourself of the commitment you made in the boardroom discussions. Remember, your relationship with God is what will generate success. Keep God part of your conversations and decisions. I am rooting for you and am excited about what God will do for you.

Never forget, your inner boardroom is a critical place for any believer in business. It is where you seek God for advice, listen for answers and walk confidently in the instruction He gives you.

RESOURCES

Manby, Joel 2012. Love Works. Zondervan

www.ingramcontent.com/pod-product-compliance
Lightning Source LLC
Chambersburg PA
CBHW052112110526
44592CB00013B/1580